Irish Saints & Sinners

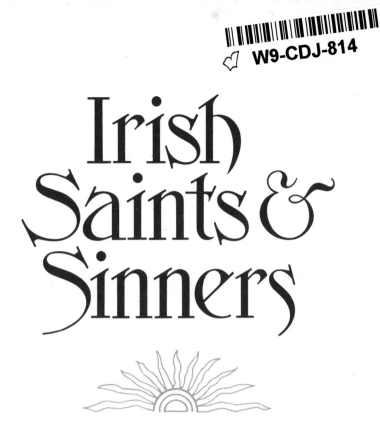

Joanne Asala
Illustrated by Marlene Ekman

STERLING PUBLISHING CO., INC.
NEW YORK

To the Wrightwood Street Gang
Rory, Fiach, Lahab, Stephanie, and Joanna
Slainte 'gus saol agat!

Library of Congress Cataloging-in-Publication Data

Asala, Joanne.
    Irish saints & sinners / Joanne Asala.
      p. cm.
    Includes index.
    ISBN 0-8069-3860-9
    1. Christian saints—Ireland—Biography. 2. Legends—Ireland.
    3. Ireland—Biography. I. Title.
    BX4659.I7A73   1995
    282'.092'2415—dc20
    [B]   95-20299
                                         CIP

10 9 8 7 6 5 4 3 2 1

Published by Sterling Publishing Company, Inc.
387 Park Avenue South, New York, N.Y. 10016
Text © 1995 by Joanne Asala
Illustrations © 1995 by Marlene Ekman
Distributed in Canada by Sterling Publishing
% Canadian Manda Group, One Atlantic Avenue, Suite 105
Toronto, Ontario, Canada M6K 3E7
Distributed in Great Britain and Europe by Cassell PLC
Wellington House, 125 Strand, London WC2R 0BB, England
Distributed in Australia by Capricorn Link (Australia) Pty Ltd.
P.O. Box 6651, Baulkham Hills, Business Centre, NSW 2153, Australia
Manufactured in the United States of America
All rights reserved

Sterling ISBN 0-8069-3860-9

I am of Ireland,
the holy land
of Ireland.

Good sir, I pray to thee,
for the sake of Holy Charity,
come and dance with me,
in Ireland.

—*Early Fourteenth Century lyric*

Contents

Glossary

aroon.	Dear one
crough.	Mountain
ovock.	Expletive, meaning "Oh, my!"
pishtrogues.	Charms
poitín.	Home-brewed whiskey
púca.	A shape-shifting Irish fairy
scrimileal.	A person of ill repute
skeeoge.	A type of kettle
sliabh.	Mountain
sthronsuch.	Lazy thing
ullagoane.	A type of wailing and moaning done at Irish wakes, usually by the women

1.
LEGENDS OF
SAINT PATRICK

St. Patrick

The Legend of the Shamrock

ONCE UPON A TIME, and a time before that, when Ireland was the land of Druids, there came a great teacher, Patrick by name, who set out to preach the word of God throughout the Emerald Isle. This saint, for of course he was a saint, was well-loved and accepted everywhere he went.

The day arrived, however, when a group of his followers came to him and admitted that it was hard for them to believe in the doctrine of the Holy Trinity.

Saint Patrick wrinkled his brow in thought, wondering how to make the people understand. He was staring at the ground when he suddenly stooped down, smiling, to pluck a leaf from the shamrock growing at his feet. He held the leaf before him, "Look closely at this living example of the Three-in-Oneness. Each petal is separate unto itself, yet together they may up the whole." The simple beauty of this explanation convinced the skeptics, and from that day on the shamrock has been revered throughout all of Ireland.

Crough Patrick

ACCORDING TO AN ancient account of the life of Saint Patrick, the holy man fasted for forty days and forty nights on the top of a mountain in what is now County Mayo, in the west of Ireland. The text goes on to say,

> *"God had said to all the saints of Ireland, past present and those to come, 'Oh, Saints, go up atop the mountain which towers and is higher than all the mountains that are towards the setting of the sun, to bless the people of Ireland, that Patrick might see the fruit of his labor.'"*

In the year 1432, a letter from the pope granted the relaxation of penances to those who made a pilgrimage to the top of Crough Patrick. To this very day, pilgrims from all over Ireland come to the mountain on the last Sunday of July. They make their way from Luisburgh or Westport, and walk on foot either of the two paths to the summit, where Masses are said. Most of the people leave from Westport, setting out in the predawn hours and climbing in the dark in order to make it to the top by sunrise. The most devout of the pilgrims have fasted for several days, and walk on the sharp rocks with their bare feet. There are a number of stations along the way where prayers are recited, and at the top they receive Holy Communion. They come in the thousands, and the paths they travel have been worn down over the centuries, so that they can be seen on the mountainside from miles around.

The Saint & the Fire-Spitter

WHEN SAINT PATRICK was at the top of the mountain known as Crough Patrick, he banished the serpents and demons into the sea, and out of Ireland forever. One demon, however, escaped the saint's curse.

This demon was known as Caorthannach, the Fire-Spitter, and it is said that she is the mother of Satan himself. Saint Patrick saw Caorthannach as she slithered and slid down the side of the mountain, and he said, "Not even *one* demon shall remain in Ireland. Not one!" When he reached the foot of the mountain, he was given a horse by one of his followers, and he set off in search of the great serpent.

Caorthannach led him on a merry chase; she spat fire all around her, burning the countryside as she rushed northward.

The serpent knew that either Saint Patrick or his horse would need water to slack their thirst, and she spat poison into all the wells as she rushed by. She was clever, that demoness, because Patrick did grow thirsty, and his horse began to slow.

At last, on the slopes of Sliabh Gamh, the Ox Mountain, he was forced to let his steed walk. Hoarse with thirst himself, he croaked out a prayer for a drink. As he prayed, his horse tripped and he was thrown from the beast's back. He landed flat on his back, and his hand banged against a rock, jarring it loose. On that spot a well sprang up beside him. Hawk's Well, it's now called. Although the waters looked stale, the holy man was glad for their cool healing powers. He drank and drank, as did his horse, and then he felt ready to face the giant serpent.

The Caorthannach had taken a different route through the mountains, and as she approached the spot where Patrick hid near Hawk's Well, the saint sprang directly in her path and cried out, "Begone, oh Serpent of Hell! Begone, Mother of Satan!" With a howl of rage the serpent was cast into the ocean, and never again has a snake been seen in Ireland. To this very day, the mark of Saint Patrick's back and his hand can be seen in the rocks near the holy well, right beside the mark of the horse's hooves.

The Island of Rabbits

---❦---

IN THE BAY OF SLIGO there is a tiny island that long ago was called Inis Coinín, the Island of Rabbits. Today it is known as Coney Island. Saint Patrick visited Inis Coinín during his missionary ventures, when he traveled the length and breadth of Ireland, teaching the people about Christianity and baptizing the Celtic people into the Church of Christ.

Wherever he went he was faced with old pagan religions, customs, and rituals. Instead of forbidding the people to practice their old ways, Saint Patrick gave these a new Christian meaning.

One of the old customs was the rule of hospitality, where strangers were welcomed as guests and given royal treatment. The people of Coney Island welcomed Saint Patrick to their shore, and listened as he preached the gospel and baptized all those who wished to be baptized. "Perhaps we may even see a church on this island," he said, and the people fervently wished this was true.

Patrick was invited to supper at the home of Berneen O'Gadhra. Berneen was in quite a frenzy when she heard that her husband had invited such an important guest to their table. "What am I to serve the man?" she cried. "We don't have anything in the house!"

Yet somehow, oddly enough, when they all sat down to eat, it was a wonderful rabbit stew that Berneen prepared.

"Delicious," pronounced the saint as he tasted the gravy. "The finest I've ever been offered." The woman blushed red, and turned away to tend her pots.

Patrick lifted his spoon to take another bite, when a

dog suddenly appeared at the door. It wagged its tail and barked twice, jumping up onto the table. "What is the meaning of this?" shouted Berneen's husband, pushing the dog back to the floor. "The beast has never acted so queerly before!"

There was a bubbling and stirring from Patrick's bowl of stew, and before anyone could say another word, out jumped a huge grey cat! It bounded out the door with the dog close on its heels.

Berneen O'Gadhra burst into tears and wept into her apron. Saint Patrick rose to his feet, knocking the offending bowl to the floor, and roared, "What are you trying to do to me, woman?"

Berneen tried to reply, but no one could understand a word she said between her sobs.

"The people of Inis Coinín must *never* forget what happened to Patrick when he visited their home. Never, *never I say*, will a church be built on this island." Hearing the gasps, and seeing the looks of dismay on the faces of the people, the kindly saint sighed and added. "But I will promise one thing to the Coinín islanders. On every Sunday of the year, from now until eternity, your people will be able to make it to the mainland for church. Neither storm nor rough seas will prevent you from hearing Mass."

Saint Patrick kept his promise. A church has never been built on Coney Island, and probably never will be. The people always cross the waters to Rosses Point, or else to Strandhill when the tide is low. No matter how bad a storm has buffeted the tiny island, it has always been possible for the islanders to reach church on Sunday, without even getting their stockings wet.

The Faerie's Question

———— ✦❋✦ ————

I F YOU GO to a funeral in County Sligo, be sure to look at the grave as the coffin draws near, and you will see the shovel and the spade which were used to dig the grave left in the shape of a cross. This custom is said to come down to us from Saint Patrick himself, and this is how it happened.

It is said by those who ought to know such things, and there aren't many of them left in Ireland anymore, that the faeries, or the *good people* as they prefer to be called, are really angels who were turned out of heaven, and who landed on their feet in this world, while the rest of their companions, who had more sin to burden them, went down farther to a blacker place.

Saint Patrick had a serving lad, a young Concobhar Draeighean by name, who was sent out one day to collect wood for a fire. He gathered a great many heavy sticks, and had quite a bundle, but being nought but a half-grown youth, he could not lift the pile.

He tugged and strained and it seemed to him that the more he struggled with the bundle, the heavier it grew. Then all at once it gave way, and Concobhar saw that a little man, one of the *good people* surely, had lifted the other end of the stack for him. They walked back to the campsite, and Concobhar said, "I am in your debt, my good sir, for I would not have been able to complete the task on my own."

"Then you should do a favor in return, Concobhar Draeighean," said the faerie with a sly grin.

"And what is it you wish?" asked Concobhar, a nervous feeling spreading through his stomach.

"Tomorrow, when Saint Patrick is saying Mass, ask him to tell you whether our souls will be saved at the last day, like the souls of good Christians. If you truly mean that you are in my debt, then bring back word of what he says as soon as you can."

The next day, during Mass, Concobhar blurted out the faerie's question. Saint Patrick raised a disdainful eyebrow at the young man, and said in a stern voice, "What are you thinking to be asking such a question in the middle of Mass? The faeries will all be lost, of course."

This answer did not settle well at all with Concobhar, and he began to tremble and shake.

After the service, Saint Patrick asked the frightened boy, "Why do you wish to concern yourself with these matters?" When he learned that his attendant must return under obligation to the *good people* to give his reply, he said, "I can only advise you this: Dig a grave for yourself both deep and wide and lay yourself down in it. At the top of the grave lay down your spade and shovel, in the shape of a cross, and this will keep back the evil demons."

"What do you think would happen if I just told them what you said?" asked Concobhar. "It sounds like an awful lot of trouble."

"If you don't do this," Patrick looked him directly in the eye, "then the *good people* will tear you limb from limb in their anger."

The next day, as Concobhar lay in the bottom of his grave, the little faerie man peered over the edge and said, "What are you doing down there, my man?"

"Oh, I'm j-j-just resting," the boy stuttered.

Dozens of other faces appeared near the edge of the grave. One of the faerie women said, "An odd place for a nap, surely. But no matter. Do you have the answer to our question? What will become of our people on the Day of Judgment?"

He hesitated a minute, and then quickly said, "They will be lost."

With that, the shrieks and howls of a million faeries rang in the air; some rushed here, and more rushed there, and some this way, and more that. A terrible storm broke out, lightning flashed and thunder roared. Concobhar trembled violently, but he did not leave the protection of the grave. As the storm abated, the faeries' cries ended in a plaintive wail.

For three long days Concobhar stayed beneath the ground, and finally he decided it was safe to come out. Ever since that time, so many years ago, all newly opened graves in Sligo have been adorned with a spade and shovel in the sign of a cross.

Saint Patrick & the Tavern Keeper

WHEN SAINT PATRICK was in Kerry, he stopped at a tavern in the town of Iveragh and called for a pint of stout. The woman went to the taps, drew him a pint, and handed it over.

"Fill it to the top!" Saint Patrick ordered. "Don't be stingy!"

She grumbled, but put another drop into the mug. Still it wasn't full.

"I said fill it to the top!" the saint repeated.

The tavern-keeper mumbled something to herself, but went over to the taps to put another drop in the mug. Still it wasn't a full pint, and Patrick sent her back four more times until he was satisfied.

"Look over your shoulder at the barrel," Saint Patrick gestured with his mug, "and tell me what you see."

The woman glanced at the barrel, and gasped in horror. "I-I-I see a huge, fat dog sitting on the barrel!" she wailed. "What does it mean?"

"It is a demon hound sent from hell. It thrives on your ill-gotten profits. Take it as a warning, woman, and mend your ways!"

Saint Patrick left the tavern, not to return to the area for another year. When he did, he stopped by the same tavern and ordered a pint of ale from the same tavern woman. This time she filled the mug to the brim.

"Do you fill every pint in this manner?" asked Patrick. The woman nodded meekly. "Well, then, look over your shoulder."

She did so, and saw a small, scrawny dog sitting on top

of the barrel. His bones were sticking out and he looked half-starved. The woman crossed her breast and breathed a prayer of thanks, vowing never again to be so stingy. She must have kept her promise, for the devil's hound was not seen in Iveragh again.

A Curse on Ireland

WHEN SAINT PATRICK was travelling through Lisdoonvarna, he stopped at the home of his friend Murphy O'Donoghue. The youngest of O'Donoghue's sons was instructed to tend to the saint's needs.

"I'm going to retire for the evening," said Patrick to the boy. "I'd like you to take care and listen to anything I may say in my sleep; I can't promise it will be pleasant, either."

"All right, sir," the boy agreed.

The saint had been asleep a good while, snoring rather loudly. He rolled over on his back and, in his sleep, yelled, "A curse on Ireland!"

The boy, who had been awake all along, replied, "If Ireland be cursed, let it only be the tips of the rushes."

Patrick tossed and turned, mumbling in his sleep, and soon began to shout again, "A curse on Ireland!"

"If Ireland is to be cursed, let it only be on the tips of a cow's horns!" the boy quickly prayed.

The good saint slept for another long while, and near cockcrow he shouted, "A curse on Ireland!"

The boy, who was near-faint with exhaustion himself, leaped up and cried, "If Ireland is to be cursed, let it be on the bottom of the furze!"

As the sun rose in the sky, Saint Patrick woke up, yawned, and stretched. His eyes fell on the boy and he asked, "Well now, lad, did I talk in my sleep?"

"You did, surely," said the boy.

"And what did I say?"

"Three times you cursed Ireland, sir," the boy answered.

"Is that right? And how did you respond?"

"At the first curse I said, 'Let it only be the tips of the rushes,' the second time I said, 'Let it be on the tips of a cow's horns,' and the third time I said, 'Let it be on the bottom of the furze!' "

"It's a smart lad you are," said the saint, "and Ireland's lucky to have you. Every priest in Ireland, I say, should have a boy help with the Mass."

And that is the reason why, to this very day, the tips of green rushes are withered and brown, why the tips of a cow's horns are black, and why the lowest branches of a furze bush are withered.

2.
LEGENDS OF
SAINT BRIDGIT

ST. BRIDGIT

Saint Bridgit's Youth

Bridgit is the name for both the Celtic fertility goddess and the Abbess of Kildare. Saint Bridgit took on many of the characteristics of her predecessor, and in Irish devotion the cult of the goddess became, almost completely unchanged, the cult of the Christian saint. Her monastery, where nine maidens tended a perpetual flame, may have started out as a pagan temple. The saint's close friendship with Bishop Conlaeth, a blacksmith, mirrors the goddess's relationship with the god Goibniu, who was also a smith. The goddess and abbess even share the same feast day, which is the first of February. Hence, the historical figure of Bridgit is lost beneath a pile of legends and miracle stories.

SAINT BRIDGIT, WHO would one day become the Abbess of Kildare, was born at sunrise on the first day of spring, to a woman of Connacht. It was a cuckoo that heralded her arrival, and an angel who blessed her and named her Bridgit, which in the old tongue means "High One" or "Fiery Arrow."

Bridgit grew up as a servant girl, just as her mother was before her, and everything she put her hand to would prosper and increase. It was she who was put in charge of the druids' sacred red-eared cow, and it was she who wove the first piece of cloth in Ireland. Ever since the time of Bridgit, Ireland has been known for its fine linens. It was Bridgit who saw to the comfort of all God's creatures, from the sheep in the fields to the birds in the trees. Her special concern, however, was for the needs of the poor.

When Bridgit reached the age of fostering, she was sent to Munster to live with her father, Dubthacht. Bridgit's father was an extremely wealthy man, and he owned a great deal of land and many costly objects. His larder was filled with more food than his household needed, and Bridgit would continuously raid it to feed the neighboring poor.

One time there came to her father's home a messenger from the High King. Food was made ready for him and for his people, and six slices of ham were given to Bridgit to broil. Now, there came into the kitchen a most miserable wretch of a wolfhound, and Bridgit, out of pity, gave him a slice of the ham. The dog still looked hungry, and the girl said, "We must fatten you up, poor dear, your ribcage can be seen through your skin." The girl fed him the remaining slices of ham.

Just then her father, Dubthacht, came into the kitchen and asked, "Do you have those pieces of ham ready for our guests?"

"Indeed she does not," said one of the other kitchen workers. "She's fed them all to the dog, she has." But when they looked onto Bridgit's plate, all six pieces of ham were there, and the honored guests enjoyed a remarkable feast.

Bridgit & the Leper

I T WASN'T LONG, however, before Bridgit's father learned that his daughter was raiding his larder, and he was furious. "No child of mine shall dare steal from me!" he bellowed. He threw her over his shoulder and tossed her into his chariot. "It is not for a pleasure-ride that you sit in my chariot. I am taking you along to sell to the King of Leinster as a slave, where you will no doubt be chained to the ovens, baking his bread."

When they reached the king's fortress, Dubthacht unstrapped his sword, leaving it on the seat beside Bridgit. It would be a sign of disrespect to face the king armed with a weapon. "Do you think you can manage to keep an eye on it?" he asked sarcastically.

As soon as he went into the fortress, a leper appeared, begging Bridgit to help him.

"Would you rather have the horse from our chariot or to be healed from your disease?" she asked.

"I would sooner be healed," said the leper, "than to rule over the whole of Ireland, for every sound man is a king."

Bridgit prayed to God, and the leper was healed. She then handed him her father's sword and said, "Take this now and sell it if you can. It should bring in enough money for you to start over again."

Meanwhile, inside the fortress, the King of Leinster was asking Dubthacht, "Why do you wish to sell your daughter?"

"She is giving away all of the wealth I have worked hard to attain," said her father angrily.

"Show her to me," said the king, "and I will make my decision."

Dubthacht noticed at once that his sword was missing, and he bellowed like a rampaging bull, "Where is my sword, girl? What have you done with it?"

"I gave it to a leper who needed it more than you," she replied.

Her father's face went purple with rage and he grabbed a stick to beat his daughter with.

The king had followed Dubthacht outside, and he now called out, "Stay your hand, and bring your daughter over here." To Bridgit he said, "Now tell me, girl, why do you steal from your father?"

"If it were within my power, I would steal all of your wealth, too, and distribute it among your poor."

The king faced Dubthacht. "Your daughter is too good for me to ever win her obedience or respect." And so, Bridgit was saved from a life of slavery.

The Love Potion

BRIDGIT WOULD GIVE herself to no man in marriage, but when she reached her sixteenth birthday, she took the veil and afterwards performed many more miracles.

There came to her one time a man by the name of Aengus O'Domhnaill who complained that his wife would no longer share his bed and was threatening to leave him. "I don't want to lose her, but want her always at my side. Do you have a spell that can restore lost love?" he asked, and there was such sadness in his eyes that Bridgit's heart melted with pity.

She took a flask of water, blessed it, and gave it to him, saying, "Take this water into your house and use it in the cooking water. Also give it to your wife to drink before going to bed."

The man did as he was told, and afterwards his wife's affections were restored. No longer did she avoid him when he was home, but always wanted to be by his side. She neglected her own duties in order to follow him to the fields; and when he needed to make a journey along the river, she stood on the bank, threatening to drown herself if she could not go along.

The man returned to Bridgit, fiercely angry, and said, "I did not ask to have a puppy following me around, I just wanted my wife's love."

"You should be careful of what you pray for," said Bridgit.

The Lake of Milk

THE SEVEN BISHOPS of Ireland arrived at Bridgit's monastery in Kildare, and the saint asked Blathnet, her cook, "Can you prepare a feast for these men?"

"I'm sorry," said Blathnet, "we do not have any food to give these fine gentlemen."

Bridgit was embarrassed and ashamed that she had nothing to serve these holiest of men, and she prayed hard to the Lord. An angel in a gown of blazing white appeared before her and said, "Bridgit, milk your cows."

"The cows have been milked twice already today," said Bridgit. "I don't think they have any more milk."

"Nevertheless, I bid you to milk your cows," insisted the angel. So Bridgit got the wooden bucket and went to the shed herself to milk. The milk filled all of the pails she had, and would have filled all of the pails in the whole of Leinster. The milk overflowed the buckets until it formed a lake that is even today known as the Lake of Milk.

3.
ENCOUNTERS
WITH THE DEVIL

The Devil & the Nutshell

O NCE UPON A TIME there was a lad named Tóibi, who went along the road to Cork cracking nuts. He found one that was terribly worm-eaten, and was about to toss it over his shoulder when he met the Devil.

They walked along in silence for a while, and then Tóibi asked, "Is it true what they say?"

"And what is that?" the Devil inquired.

"That you can make yourself as small as you like, so small that you could even fit through the eye of a needle."

"Yes," the Devil grinned, "it is not a difficult task."

"I don't believe it; you'll have to prove it to me," the boy said.

"You want proof?" The Devil raised his eyebrows. "My word is not good enough?"

"Considering your reputation, no. I want to see you crawl into this nut, if you can," Tóibi said.

No sooner did he say so than the Devil did it. He shrunk down until he was nearly invisible, and crawled into the worm hole. Tóibi sealed the hole with a pebble and put the nut in his pocket.

"Safe enough, now," laughed the lad, patting his pocket.

When he reached Cork City, he stopped at the home of a friend of his who was a smithy. "Can you crack this nut for me?" he asked.

"Easily asked, easily done," said the smith. He took the smallest hammer he had, placed the nut on the anvil, and gave it a whack; it didn't break.

"Perhaps you need a bigger hammer," Tóibi suggested. And so the smith took a hammer that was a little bit larger and struck the nut again. Still it didn't break.

"Give me my sledgehammer," the smith growled, angry now. He gave the nut such a blow with the hammer that it shattered into a thousand pieces, splitting the anvil in two and sending the roof right off the building.

The smith pushed a lock of hair from his eyes and said, "The Devil must've been in that nut."

"He must have," grinned Tóibi.

Moling & the Devil

ONCE, WHEN SAINT MOLING was praying in church, he saw a man walk in wearing a gold-trimmed robe of costly purple velvet. The man smiled broadly and held out his arms to embrace Moling, but the holy man stayed where he was by the altar.

"Why don't you come and welcome me home?" the man asked.

"Who are you?" demanded Moling.

"Why, I am Christ," the man smiled, "the Son of God."

Moling raised a single eyebrow and grunted in derision, "I doubt that, truly."

"Why is that?" The man slowly lowered his arms. "You do not recognize me?"

"Not as you are now," said Moling, "no. When Christ

walks among his servants, he does not wear the fine dress of a king, but rather comes in the guise of a leper, or a beggar, or a poor little child."

"Ah, I see!" A glint lit the stranger's eyes. "Who is it that you think I am?"

Moling sighed and said, "I suppose you must be the Devil, here to tempt me. Well, go about it quickly and leave me alone, I have much to do this day."

The man made no move to leave, and Moling raised a copy of the gospels, as if to strike him. "All right!" the Devil howled in pain, and fell writhing to the floor, the rich garments fading away to reveal his true nature. "You win! I've come here to ask your blessing."

"You shall not have it," sniffed Moling. "What kind of a fool are you to ask for it?"

"Then give me the full impact of your curse!" the Devil pleaded, jumping to his feet. "I await your foul words of banishment."

"What good will that do? The venom and sting of the curse will be on my lips. Now go away and try your tricks on someone less cunning. I've grown weary of your presence." Moling then turned his back on the Devil and returned to his prayers.

The Devil realized that any further discourse was pointless, and he left Moling's church, never to return.

O'Hara & the Hell Hound

CONOR O'HARA WAS a seafaring man, just as his father and grandfather were before him. He lived with his brother Liam, on the rare occasions when he lived on land, in the town of Rosslare. One evening, as he was returning from the harbor, he ran into a great black dog. He knew from the red glow in the creature's eyes that the beast was not of this world.

The dog was larger than any dog he had seen before, and was as black as coal soot. He had a link of chains around his neck which rattled and clattered as he charged at Conor.

The poor man was frozen in terror, and was convinced that the creature was going to grab him by the neck for his sins and drag him down to the darkest pits of Hell.

The dog got nearer, the razor-sharp teeth catching the light of the moon, his roar like the waves breaking against the rocks, and the sailor cried out, "May the Lord God have mercy on my soul!"

Satan's hound was about to sink his teeth into Conor's neck, but as soon as the name of God was spoken aloud, the creature stopped dead in his tracks and howled out his anguish.

"Curses to you, Conor O'Hara. You have won this time, but I won't forget you! We'll be watching!" With those words, the creature from Hell howled again and disappeared in a cloud of red smoke.

Conor, seeing that he had escaped a fate worse than death, ran home to his brother's house and banged and pounded on the door. When Liam opened the door, Conor fell into a faint.

What did Conor learn from his experiences? It is said in Rosslare that Conor O'Hara went to church the very next Sunday, something that was very much out of character for the man, and he continued to make the church his very first stop whenever he returned to shore.

The Demon Cat

ONCE UPON A TIME there lived in Galway a woman named Maura O'Byrne. She was the wife of a fisherman, and as her husband always had good luck at sea, Maura always had plenty of fish stored away in the house to take to market. But wouldn't you know it, a great black cat used to sneak into the storeroom at night and eat the best and finest fish. So Maura kept a big stick at her side, and decided to keep watch. But, alas, she always fell asleep and never saw the cat come in.

One afternoon, however, as she and her daughters were cooking the evening meal, the house became quite dark, the walls shook, and the door was thrown open as if by the blast of a storm. In walked the black cat. It hissed at the woman and then went straight to the fire to sit down.

"Why, surely that's the Devil himself," said the youngest daughter. "What other creature would act so bold and make such an entrance?"

"You'll soon learn to mind your manners properly," hissed the cat, and, jumping at the startled girl, scratched her face. The blood flowed freely from the cuts onto her apron.

"There now," laughed the cat, "you will watch your tongue the next time a gentleman comes calling."

The cat jumped up onto the table and examined the most recent catch of fish. "What, no salmon today?" he asked. "Salmon is my favorite; I am very disappointed, although I suppose this will have to do."

By this time Maura had had enough of the cat and his arrogant ways, and she raised her stick shouting, "Away with you, you nasty, stinking beast!" She dealt him such a blow that it would have broken his back if he weren't a demon. "You won't be eating any more of *my* fish, so you won't!"

The cat only grinned at the frustrated woman, and bent down to tear the head off of one of the fish. "You think you can stop me, human woman?" he sneered between bites. "Your threats mean nothing!"

"But I'll help, so I will!" shouted the youngest daughter, picking up a heavy cast-iron skillet. Her sister did the same, and the three women attacked the cat and struck blows hard enough to kill him, if he were an ordinary house cat.

The demon cat began to spit fire. "How dare you!" he howled, and he tore at their arms and legs with his claws until the blood flowed freely and the frightened women ran shrieking from the house.

Yet Maura O'Byrne was not one to be bested by a cat, not even a demon cat. She soon returned with a bottle of holy water, and, peering in through the open door, she saw that the cat was still on the table, calmly eating the fish. She crept up quietly behind the beast, so quietly that he suspected nothing, and threw the holy water on its back.

Oh, how that cat did howl and spit! A dense cloud of black smoke filled the cabin, and all Maura could see were the two red eyes of the demon, burning like coals of fire. Finally the smoke cleared away, and all that was left of the demon cat was a shriveled and charred mass. Maura picked up the remains of the cat with her tongs and tossed them out onto the ash heap. From that time on, the fish remained untouched and safe from harm, for once such an evil has been thwarted, it will not return again.

If You Sup with the Devil, Be Sure to Carry a Long Spoon

THE DEVIL AND the tax-collector set out for Cork one fine summer morning in order to settle a bet they had made the night before over a jug of *poitín,* that rare old mountain dew. They wished to know who could gather the best load by sunset, and neither one was to collect anything unless it was freely offered by the giver.

They soon passed a house, and they heard the poor farm wife cry out to her lazy daughter, "Oh, Musha, the Devil take you for a lazy *sthronsuch* of a girl! Do you intend to leave your bed at all today?"

"Oh, ho!" said the tax-collector to Old Nick. "I think I see a job for you!"

"Ovock!" replied the other. "The mother did not mean those words from her heart. We must continue on."

At the next cabin they passed, they heard the woman of the house as she called to her husband from the cow pasture, "Oh, doom and gloom to you, my man! You never brung them pigs, and they are rootin' away in the potato drills! The Devil run to Belfast with them!"

"There's another windfall in your lap!" laughed the tax-collector.

The Devil only shook his horns wistfully and said, "No, it cannot be. It was not from the heart." They continued on like this, with ever so many things offered to the Evil One, and he never taking a one. Nor was the tax-collector offered even the smallest serving of buttermilk, and at last the sun was near the edge of Cooliagh. They were just passing Monamolin when they came across a poor woman straining her supper in a *skeeoge* beside her cabin door. She saw the two visitors and shouted, "Lord save us! It's the tax-collector! Run away with him!"

"Ah," sighed the Devil, "I've got a bite at last!"

"No! No!" the tax-man shouted. "She didn't mean that from the heart!"

"Indeed she did, and it was from the very foundation stones of her soul that it came. No help for it, surely, so into the bag with you!" The Devil opened his big black bag, tossed the poor soul inside, and shut it with a click. And whether or not the Devil was ever seen strolling along that same path none could say, but sure it is that the tax-man was never seen in those parts again.

4.
TALES OF THE CLERGY

The Crowza Stones

FATHER ROWAN FOLEY lived in Wexford, and, finding little enough to do there except to say prayers over fishing nets and attend old women in their final hour, he decided to visit his cousin Keverne, a monk who lived across the waters in Cornwall.

Keverne was a hermit, and usually liked to be alone, but he welcomed his cousin with open arms and the two passed the evening in drink and conversation. They had tumbler after tumbler of sweet honey mead, toasting their families and friendship, when Father Rowan noticed the fine gold chalice that Keverne was drinking from.

"That is indeed the most beautiful thing I've ever seen," said Rowan. "Wherever did you get it?"

"It was given to me by a merchant in Dyffed when I tended his wife's sickbed."

Father Rowan grew jealous as Keverne poured himself another drink, and he thought, "I will never receive such a gift from my parishioners." Shortly afterwards, he took leave of his cousin, promising to return soon.

It wasn't long before Keverne missed his cup, and after searching for it high and low, he was forced to conclude that Rowan had stolen it. "My own flesh and blood has deceived me!" he roared. "He will pay for it, he will!" He stormed out of his hut in pursuit of the wayward priest.

As he passed by Crowza Down, he scooped up a number of the iron stones which littered the ground. In the distance he could see Rowan, and he hollered, "I know you have my cup, Rowan, you thief! Don't you take another step!"

The priest turned around and saw that he was discovered, but didn't stop; in fact, he increased his pace, hoping to reach his boat before his cousin reached him.

"I warned you, Rowan!" Keverne called out as he threw one of the rocks at his cousin. It grazed the priest's head and landed before him with a reverberating thud.

"Are you crazy?" shouted the priest, looking over his shoulder and ducking as another stone came flying toward him. "Okay, okay, I'm sorry! Take back your blasted chalice!" He untied his purse and tossed the golden vessel to the ground. Then he leaped into the boat and paddled furiously away.

Keverne, in his anger, continued throwing the rocks at his cousin, cursing him with all his might. The stones remain there to this day, quite unlike the stones around them, but obviously the same type of stones as those found at Crowza Down. So heavy are they that only a holy man or a demon could possibly have lifted them.

The Tobacco Prayer

NOLLAIG TOBIN, RECENTLY home from the seminary, was walking down the streets of his home village when an angel of the Lord appeared to him and said, "You are damned, as is everyone in your flock, because of the sins of your mother."

"My mother?" Nollaig blinked uncomprehendingly. "My mother is the most God-fearing of Christian women. What sins has she committed?"

"For twenty years has she smoked a pipe of tobacco, and never once has she said the tobacco prayer. Just as one ought to be thankful to God for his meals, so ought one be thankful for the good things in life."

"Bad luck to us!" exclaimed the priest. "Is there anything that can be done?"

"You must tell your mother what I have said, and you must tell her this as well. That unless she is willing to undergo the death that has been chosen for her, she will never see the Golden Gates of Heaven, nor will any of her family step through those gates."

"What death is that?" asked Father Nollaig.

"She must throw herself off the Cliffs of Moher and into the sea."

The priest went to his mother's cottage with a heavy load on his heart. He pulled his chair up close to the fire and there were lines of grief etched all across his face.

"What is troubling you, my son?" his mother asked. "Has something happened to disturb you?"

"Ah, there's nothing wrong that a little sleep won't cure," said he. "Can you kindle the pipe for me, Mother? I'd like a bit of tobacco before bed."

"I'll kindle it for you, and welcome," said his mother.

"I didn't know, my son, that you smoked the pipe."

"Ah, perhaps a little whiff now and then would help lift my spirits." He watched carefully as his mother prepared the pipe, hoping that she would say the tobacco prayer, but she did not.

Then Father Nollaig told his mother of what the angel had said, and she threw herself onto her knees and prayed to God, "Thank you, dear Lord, for choosing this death for me. I will gladly suffer for my sins."

The mother bathed herself and brushed her hair until it shone. Then she and her son travelled to the edge of the Cliffs of Moher. She was about to throw herself over the edge when the angel appeared before them, saying, "You and your family have been forgiven for their sins because of your honest repentance. Go home now, good woman, and do not forget to offer up the tobacco prayer every time you fill your pipe."

Never afterwards did Meg Tobin forget to offer up her prayer of thanks to God and to the Virgin, just as the people of the West still offer up the same prayer to this day.

The Mad Priest & His Flock

THERE WAS A man named John Connors, who lived near Killarney, and who owned a mill near the crossroads. One night, as he was working late, a strange man with black wooly hair opened the door and stood at the threshold, not stepping in.

John wiped his hands on his apron and stepped forward. "God bless you and welcome this night. What brings you here at such a late hour? I did not hear a wagon approach."

The stranger did not return the greeting, but said in a low, hollow voice, "If you had a choice, John Connors, would you sooner have your son or your wife lose their wits?"

The miller, thinking nothing of the question, grinned and said, "My wife is surely the most sensible woman in the parish, and my son is at seminary and will shortly come back to us as a priest. There's no fear of madness in either of them."

"Only time will tell, then," said the stranger, and without another word he turned and left.

John's son came home the very next week and read his first Mass that Sunday in the village church. It was also to be his last sermon there, as fate would have it, for that very evening a madness crept over the young man, and he tore off his nightclothes and ran about the village as bare as a bullfrog, carrying with him a large book written in Latin.

He was finally calmed down and coaxed to dress, although he would not return to his father's house. Nor would he sup on the porridge his mother gave him, refusing everything except watercress and wild onions. Each night he would sleep in his father's mill, using the great book for a pillow, and each day found him in the fields, reading to the sheep from the same great book. Oddly enough, the sheep would gather at his feet as if they understood every word he said.

One of the village maids spied on him, and she heard him tell the flock, "You are all without sin, every one of you, and you are all under the care of the great Lamb of God. You have plenty of green grass and fresh herbs to nibble on, and each of you has a fine, warm coat to keep you dry."

The maid could hardly contain her astonishment, and she later told the other villagers how the priest preached to the flock of sheep about the Son of God, and the hardships He suffered for the sins of man.

The father, hearing this, said to his wife, "Katie, our son has completely lost his wits. We should take him to Dublin to see a doctor." He took hold of a lantern and went with his wife to the mill. As his wife opened the door, they saw spilling out a cold, bright light, brighter than the sun, and their poor, mad son lying sound asleep, the book tucked comfortably under his head as a pillow. The parents did not dare go inside, however, for golden rams with curling silver horns stood on either side of the young man, keeping watch as he slumbered.

The Priest of Donaghedy

A CERTAIN PRIEST LIVING in Donaghedy used to go out of his house a few steps every night in order to relieve himself before going to sleep. But one night when he went outside, he was met by a strange little man.

"You can't possibly know," said the man in a whiskey-smooth voice, "what a terrible nuisance you are to me and my family."

"Whatever do you mean?" asked the priest, not at all surprised to be addressed in such a manner.

"My house is right below your feet. Just take hold of my hand and you will see for yourself."

The priest clasped the hand of the other, and looked down at the ground. It was as if the grass were not even there, and he could see straight into a tiny house.

"My roof is not completely water-tight, either, if you know what I mean," said the stranger without a trace of humor.

"I'm frightfully sorry," said the red-faced priest.

"If you promise to take your evening walk on the other side of your house, I can promise you a great treasure."

The priest promised to do so, and was led to a great cache of gold, which he used to feed the poor of his parish.

5.
TALES OF
MUSICIANS

Saint Moling & the Musician's Harp

SAINT MOLING NEVER allowed himself the pleasure of music and song, declaring it to be "the pastime of the idle." He usually forbad any musicians in his presence.

One spring day a young man with hair of gold came to Moling's monastery with a harp slung over his shoulder. All of the monks were at the evening meal, except for Moling, who had chosen to fast instead. One of the monks asked the young man what he wanted.

"I was hoping you would share your meal with me, and in return I will play for you on my harp."

"We freely offer what we have," said the monk. "There's no need for payment."

"Nevertheless, I would like to play for you anyway," the young man insisted. He took out his harp and played many a fine song, both sad and merry, for the delighted monks. At last he asked, "Which one of you men is Moling, whose holiness I have heard of in my far-off city."

"He's in the chapel," said one of the older monks. "Every other day he chooses to fast, and he can always be found there." When the young musician had finished eating, he walked towards the church. The monks shook their heads sadly, for they knew full well that Moling hated to hear music of any kind.

When the musician entered the tiny chapel, Moling was deep in prayer. The young man settled next to the altar and began to play. Without looking up, and without halting his prayer, the good saint took from his pocket two balls of wax, and stuffed them into his ears.

The harpist smiled to himself, and continued to play. To Moling's amazement, he felt the wax in his ears begin to melt and trickle down his neck. Much as he tried to gather the drippings and stuff them back in his ears, they just continued to run.

He looked suspiciously at the musician, who now took from his sack a small stone. He scraped it across the strings of his harp, and they gave an awful wailing, as if of a soul in agony. Moling found it impossible to listen, and he begged the musician to stop.

At last the young man with the hair of gold replaced the stone in his sack, and played on the harp as sweetly as the song of the nightingale. Moling felt a great joy spread through him. At last he asked, "Are you the Devil, come to tempt me again? Or are you one of Heaven's angels?"

The young man smiled to himself and said in a voice as sweet as honey, "For that you must make up your own mind. When I scraped my stone across the strings, it made the noise of the Devil. And when I played it with my fingers it made the sound of a heavenly choir. Music, like food or drink, like work or play, can be a conduit for evil, or a source for good."

The young musician packed the harp back into its case, and he left Moling to ponder his words. From that time on, the good saint allowed all musicians to play at the monastery, and he gave up his excessive fasting except for, of course, the Holy Days. His fellow monks could not help but notice a change in the man, although they dared not comment upon it for fear of facing his sharp tongue.

The Satanic Piper

M ANY HUNDREDS AND hundreds of years ago, on a Saturday evening it was, a certain Cathal O'Neill took his young bride, Mary, along with their relatives and friends, to the ruins of an old church to celebrate their nuptials. Here they feasted and danced until the bells from the distant village tolled the hour of midnight. The piper, a right pious man, refused to play any longer.

"I'll make it worth your while," said Cathal, reaching for his wallet. "The guests aren't ready to leave yet."

"Please," the bride begged prettily, "it is my wedding day."

"I cannot," the piper said sadly. "Not on the Sabbath."

"Well," Mary stamped her little foot. "I shall *not* be spoken to in such a way by a beggar like you. I *will* have a piper, even if I have to go to the lowest regions of Hell to find one."

Scarcely had she spoken these words when an old man with a long white beard stepped out from the shadows. "I am a piper, and I will play for you," he said.

The old man, who was none other than the Devil himself, buckled his pipes around his middle and started with a slow and sad air.

"That's no music for a wedding!" shouted Cathal. His guests quickly agreed.

"It's dancing music you want?" cackled the old man. "Then it's dancing music you shall have!" Without another word the piper swung into a lively reel.

The host now began to dance. They soon found themselves whirling around the demon piper so fast and so furious that they were more than a bit willing to stop and rest. Their shoes, however, had a mind of their own, and refused to stop dancing to the Devil's tune.

The old man threw off his disguise, and the people gasped in horror to see that it was Satan they had invited into their midst. They begged and pleaded for mercy, but to no avail.

The sun was just beginning to peek over the horizon, a warning to the Devil that he must soon depart, and he said to the crowd, "I leave you here as a monument to my power and to your wickedness, a monument that will last until the end of time."

The Devil then vanished, and the villagers, on rising in the morning, found the field strewn with boulders. The stones were set in rings, just like the rings of dancers.

Conflicting Interests

T HERE WAS ONCE a piper in County Leitrim who was known as Sean Thornton. Much of Sean's money was earned from his playing at a crossroads every Sunday afternoon. Whether it was because of his remarkable music, or his pleasant manner, or the opportunity for the young folk to get better acquainted, a large crowd gathered at the crossroads. Word of Sean's prosperity finally reached the ears of the parish priest.

Father Michael happened along to the crossroads one Sunday afternoon and stood nearby, watching the proceedings. It was just out of curiosity, it should be told, and not out of malicious intent.

The piper had dug a hole in the ground next to where he sat, and into this hole the young men would toss their coppers after each dance. The pastor was soon convinced that the stories of Sean's wealth had not been exaggerated, and he decided that there must be an end made to these dances, and soon. It was positively sinful that so much money should be wasted on frivolity when it could be put to better use. There were so many poor in the parish to feed and clothe!

Father Michael went up to Sean, and in no uncertain terms said, "I'm afraid you will have to leave this parish, and take your music elsewhere."

"What do you mean?" asked Sean incredulously.

"You're taking in more money than I take in at the offering. There is not enough money in this parish for the both of us."

"I'm not to blame for that, surely," said the piper. "It's your father's fault, if anybody's."

"My father's?" the priest said in surprise. "How could he have anything to do with this, might I ask?"

"He had everything to do with this," winked Sean. "He ought to have made a piper out of you instead of a priest!"

The Power of Music

AT THE FUNERAL of Father Owen Cullen, the most disliked man in the parish, a strange and unexpected thing happened. Nobody but the family had arrived to mourn the passing of the man, and, prompted by a desperation that arose from grief and humiliation, the priest's brother ran into the house for his pipes, climbed into the cart, and took his seat on the coffin. There he buckled on his pipes and struck up such a haunting lamentation that it rivalled the *ullagoane* of any grief-stricken widow.

The wailing of the pipes allowed the priest's family to voice their sorrow, and naturally enough they attracted everyone within hearing. Not a soul who witnessed the procession was unmoved, and by the time the funeral cart reached the gates of the cemetery, a large crowd of mourners were weeping and wailing and striking their breasts. It was the largest funeral the town had ever seen.

6.
CREATURES
OF THE
SUPERNATURAL

The Púca Who Built the Church

A CARPENTER, WHOSE name was Rory, was contracted to build a church in Carlow, where he lived. But whatever his crew built during the day collapsed again at night. This made Rory very discouraged and disgusted with himself, because his professional reputation was on the line, after all, and he did not know what to do.

On the third morning, when he again found the church in ruins, he fell to cursing. "Ruin and damnation! What is the meaning of this?" he howled. "How can I complete the task I swore to do? Never before has Rory Ó Murchu gone against his word, and I won't be starting now! But what am I to do?"

At this a tall, thin man appeared at his side. Both of his hands were covered by mittens, and he gave Rory a toothy smile. "I can build your church for you, Ó Murchu," he laughed.

"Can you now?" The carpenter shook his head in disbelief. "If you can manage that, I'd be most surprised, but also very grateful."

"I can build your church for you," the man repeated, "but you must promise me something in return."

"And what is that?" asked Rory suspiciously.

"I ask one of three things: either the sun or the moon or your heart, which even now beats in your chest."

Well, the carpenter discussed this proposal with his men, "I don't think that this beanpole of a man can accomplish what all of us could not. But let's take him up on his offer. It might make a good bit of sport."

The stranger started to work, although he did not remove his mittens. The crew watched in amazement as the building was quickly constructed, but the carpenter grew nervous because he realized that he would have to give the man his heart. There was no way he would ever be able to get the sun or the moon.

The tall man finished his task without even working up a sweat and said, "I will release you from your bargain if you can guess my name."

"Is it Aengus? Is it Gareth. Is it Hugh? Seamus? Jeffrey? Cian?" the carpenter asked hopefully.

"No!" chuckled the tall man with glee, giving Rory another toothy grin. "It's not any of those names!"

"Martin!" shouted the carpenter desperately. "Is it Martin? Rónán? Darragh?"

"You'll never guess," said the stranger, "even if you sat there until the end of time. I don't have that long to wait, and so I'll be back tomorrow to collect on your debt!"

The carpenter did not wish to lose his life, and so he decided to escape. He took off in the middle of the night, and headed into the hills. He walked and walked, and when he had walked for many miles he walked some more. When he grew tired, he sat down near a hill. The sun was just beginning to rise.

The sound of crying voices came from within the hill, and then the voice of a tired old woman said, "Hush now, my darlings, hush. Tonight your father Goibniu [the Smith] will come home, and he will bring you the sun, the moon, or perhaps the heart of that foolish carpenter in the village." The hillside opened up, and out danced four young colts followed by a mare, all as black as coal. In that instant Rory knew what they were, and what the strange man was as well.

"No wonder he always wore gloves!" he exclaimed. "That shape-shifting horse-fairy, that *púca,* can not become completely human! His hands remain hooves!" What wonderful luck to have come across this hillside, he thought, and with his newfound knowledge he rushed back to Carlow. On his way he met the tall, thin man.

"You want me to give you my heart," Rory said, looking properly scared. "What will you use it for?"

"To season my children's soup!" the *púca* said. "But you can still go free if you can guess my name."

"Is it Fergus? Miles? Aaron? Kyras? No? Well then, it must be Goibniu!"

"What!?!" the *púca* shouted in disbelief. "Who told you, *who told you?*" Before the carpenter's startled eyes the man's form seemed to shiver and melt away, and in his place stood a jet-black stallion, rearing up on his hind legs. "It is lucky you are, Rory, for I would have surely ripped your heart from your breast!"

In his anger the *púca* tore a path through the forest; he knocked over trees and dug up bushes, he kicked aside boulders and trampled on flowers. By the time he got to the church, he tore out a stone from the north side. He would have torn down the whole church, if he could, but his strength was spent. Today the people of Carlow say that each November, when the *púca* roams the countryside, you can hear him howling out his frustration for his unfinished task.

The Good People

———◆※◆———

There was once a wide-spread belief throughout Europe and Ireland that the faeries and other supernatural creatures are descendents of either Lucifer's followers or Eve's children. Sometimes the legends say that the good people are descended from Adam's first wife, Lilith.

WHEN THE GOOD Lord chased Adam and Eve from the Garden of Eden, they did not have much reason for happiness. And yet, they loved each other dearly, and had a great many children together.

One day the Lord visited Eve while she was bathing her children in the river near their home. Eve was fiercely ashamed that they had so many children, and in her awe and wonder she hid away all those children that she had not yet washed.

The Lord looked at the freshly scrubbed children, and He praised Eve because they were so beautiful. "But tell me, Eve, *aroon*," He said, "are all of your children here?"

"Yes, yes they are," she said.

"You don't have any others?"

"N-n-no," Eve replied in an unsteady voice. "All of the children that Adam and I have you see before you."

"I see," said the Lord, nodding to Himself. "Then let those children that you've hidden from me be hidden from all men. Let those children become the *good people*, and keep to the hills."

And, to this day, the children of Eve have remained in the secret places of the wild, keeping hidden amongst the trees and rocks, waiting for the day when they might return to the world of men and women.

The Witches of Anglesey

THE NOTORIOUS WITCHES of Llanddona, on the Isle of Anglesey, came along with their husbands by boat. They had been expelled from their native Ireland by the good Saint Patrick, allowed to take nothing but the clothes on their backs. When their oarless and rudderless boat approached the Welsh coastline, the people tried to drive them back with prayers and with threats. The tides brought them to shore anyway, and when they landed on the sandy beach, they commanded that a spring of pure water appear to quench their thirst.

The strangers were allowed to stay, but even then they were viewed with suspicion by some and feared by most. The men kept to themselves, smuggling to earn a living, and the women were either forced to beg or were sought to cast spells and charms. They were the best midwives, and only at the time of a birth would the people dare let the witches come into their homes.

The power of witchcraft was thought to pass from mother to daughter, and the fear of them was so great that it was seldom that a father would allow his son to marry one of the foreign women. To this day, when a red-haired child is born on the Isle of Anglesey, it is said to be descended from the cast-out Irish witches.

The Mermaid of Inishturk

IT WAS MANY and many a year ago, before the great pirate queen Grace O'Malley took her first tottering steps, that a priest of Inishturk went down to the sea to gather mussels.

The water was at low tide, and the priest, clambering over the rocks with his bucket and shovel, suddenly stopped at the sight before him. Stranded on the beach by the retreating tide was a young and very beautiful sea-nymph. Mermaids are always described as beautiful, it's true, but this one really was, with hair the color of a sunset at sea and eyes as blue as the ocean's depths. She was weeping bitterly.

"What is wrong, my pretty one?" asked the priest softly, so as not to startle her.

"I was combing out my hair, and did not notice the tide retreating," sniffed the mermaid. It is not known what language the sea people speak between themselves, but this one spoke in perfect Irish.

"That was very vain of you, was it not?" asked the priest. A strange feeling swept through him as he gazed at the mermaid, and he could not help but sweep her under his arm and carry her back to his home. He filled a trough with saltwater and set her in it.

"Please let me go, oh, please!" begged the mermaid, but the priest pulled up a chair next to the trough, and sat beside her, dazzled by her beauty.

The mermaid thrashed her tail in rage, and she hollered, "I place a curse on you now! I swear that no child shall ever be born under the roof of this house!" She did not understand that this man was a priest; it is doubtful if she even knew what a priest was.

The priest, however, seemed to wake from his stupor, and he hurriedly carried the mermaid back to the sea.

For five hundred years the curse has hung over the heads of the parish priests, one after the other. Yet what good is such a curse against a man of the cloth?

"Surely now, it's a lucky man you are, to be cursed so," said one old priest to his successor.

"Why?" asked the younger man, blushing furiously. "I'm not sure what you mean."

"Well, you won't be able to get any of the parish girls in trouble, will you now?"

7.
THE IRISH ABROAD

The Blarney Stone of Saint Brynach

———◆◆◆———

S AINT DAVID, THE PATRON saint of Wales, had a friend named Brynach. Brynach was a monk from Ireland who spent long periods of time praying and meditating in his tiny cell. He was known far and wide for his understanding of animals and other living creatures and, like many Irishmen, he had a gift of the blarney as well.

Saint David often stopped to visit his friend at the church in Nevern on his journeys through the Welsh countryside, and one day Brynach spotted him carrying an intricately carved Celtic cross. The stone was marvelous to behold, a full thirteen feet high and two feet wide, with an interlocking pattern of cords and loops carved into the surface and topped with the distinctive wheeled cross.

Impressed that David was able to carry the cross by himself, he asked, "What power is it that aids you, my friend? That stone must be heavy."

"It isn't really," said David. "My burden is lightened by the powers of Heaven."

"What do you intend to do?" Brynach asked.

"I am taking it to the monastic community at Llanddewi Brefi. It's a memorial to myself."

"I must say I wouldn't have expected that from you," Brynach said, frowning sternly at his friend.

"Whatever do you mean?" asked David, genuinely puzzled.

"Isn't it rather arrogant of you to carry around a stone that is dedicated to yourself?"

"Well . . ." David hesitated.

"Besides," Brynach continued in true Irish style, "you could seriously harm yourself carrying such a great burden. Llanddewi Brefi is a long way off."

"You are right, Brynach," David said. "For the good of my soul, not to mention my back, I think I will leave the cross with you."

"I couldn't possibly let you do that!" the other man protested.

"No, I insist," said David, and so he left the stone in Nevern. There it remains to this day, known as *Saint Brynach's Cross.*

The Legend of Saint Deglan

WHEN SAINT DEGLAN was returning from a trip to Rome, he accidentally left his bell upon a rock in the harbor. The ship pulled out to sea, with the bell left behind.

It wasn't until Deglan reached the coast of Ireland that he remembered his bell, and he thought of the old saying "There's not much good in a cleric without a bell." So he prayed to God that his bell would be delivered to him.

At the end of Deglan's prayer, what should be seen swimming behind the boat but that selfsame bell, and the rock with it, too. The rock followed the ship all the way into the harbor at Ardmore, and up onto the shore as well. And there the rock can be seen to this day, situated atop two smaller rocks.

Why the Irish Came to America

THE KING OF ENGLAND wanted to get married, but he could not find a maid to suit him. He turned the kingdom over to his brother, and travelled through the West Country in search of a wife. He came to a desolate stretch of beach along the southern coast, and there he met a monk from Ireland. The two became good friends, often hunting and fishing together.

One day as they were fishing along the shore of a lovely little lake, the monk asked, "Have you given up your search for a wife, sire?"

"No, I haven't," sighed the king. "I just don't know where to look anymore."

"You could go to Ireland," said the monk. "That's where the world's most beautiful maidens are. I had to leave the island because they were too much of a temptation for me!"

"I may just do that!" laughed the king. As they chuckled together, they suddenly saw three snow-white swans glide smoothly across the lake. The king wanted to catch one for their evening meal, but the monk held up his arm.

"Those aren't really swans," he said. "They're three girls, sisters, I suppose, who come down to this lake every day for a swim."

"You don't say!" said the king. "How could we capture them, do you wonder?"

"The only way I know of is to take their clothes," said the monk. "You don't really intend to play such a wicked trick, do you?"

"Just watch and keep quiet," the king said, giving him

a conspirator's wink. He slipped up the bank of the lake and stole the three girls' clothes before they knew what happened.

When the swan girls swam to shore and saw what the king had done, they begged for their clothes. But the king said, "No, not unless I can go with you, too."

"All right," the women agreed. The oldest swan girl told the king to get on her back, and away they flew. They travelled a long way until they came to a mountain, and there the king was dropped. The second sister caught him up and carried him across the mountain, after which she, too, dropped him. The youngest sister caught him and carried him the rest of the way. It was the youngest swan the king wished to marry.

When they reached the home of the three sisters, they let fall their swan outfits, and the king could not tell the maidens apart. "You must be able to chose the correct one," one of the girls said.

The youngest girl gave him a sign, however. When her sisters weren't looking, she gave the king a wink. The two were married soon after, and for a time were very happy. But the king wanted to go back to England.

"You can't leave here," his wife protested, "if you do you will surely die." The king kept on insisting, however, and at last his wife constructed a flying ship to carry him back.

The king said, "I promise you, dear wife, that I won't leave the ship. I just want one final glimpse of England."

When the king got to England, he forgot all about what he had promised his wife. He jumped out of the ship and stepped on land. The Angel of Death was waiting for him.

"Don't take me," begged the king. "There are many old men around here, I'm still young and strong."

"It's you I want," said the Angel of Death, grabbing hold of the king's collar.

The king saw that there was little use in arguing with Death, so he sighed and said, "I'll get in that little box of yours, Death, if you crawl in first. I'm frightened."

"All right," agreed Death. "There's nothing to be afraid of."

When Death crawled into the box, the King of England shut the lid tight and fastened him in so that he could not get out. Then the king got back into his flying ship and returned to his wife.

When the king returned to his mountain home, he told his wife and her sisters what had happened, and he started to open the box to prove his story.

"Don't open the box!" His wife held out her arm. "If you do, we'll all die."

They didn't know what to do with Death, but a big storm rose on the ocean, and they took the box with Death in it and dropped it into the sea. The box floated a long time until it reached Ireland, and was washed to shore. Several men pulled the box from the water and wondered what could be inside. Two big, burly men got their sledgehammers and broke the box open. The Angel of Death flew out of the box in a rage, and killed every man that was there, and he continued to sweep over the countryside, killing people all over Ireland. That was why many Irishmen left Ireland to go to America.

Give the Devil His Due

EDWIN JAMES LIVED in the Appalachian foothills of northern Georgia, just as his father did before him. His father's father had sailed from Ireland before the great famines. He had been a belligerent, often drunken fellow, but he was smart, too. He taught his children that it made more economic sense to convert their grain into alcohol. "Twenty bushels of corn will only bring you six dollars," he'd say. "Make it into corn whiskey and you can earn twenty-six." He passed on his love of moonshine to his grandson, along with his set of pipes.

Edwin was a fine player, despite his reputation for being a wild fellow who was a wee bit too fond of the drink. His pipes were his prize possession and many was the starlit night that he could be found on the hickory stump by his back porch, playing jigs to the moon.

One night he was playing for himself, long after his wife and sons had gone to bed, and every now and then he would take a swig from his jug and gaze up at the heavens. He was startled when one of the stars fell from the sky and landed right in his yard! There was a flash of black light, and a man with an oak-wood case stood facing him. He brushed some star-dust from his shoulders.

"Who might you be?" Edwin asked.

"The Devil," the man replied with a chuckle.

"Go on, now, quit your kidding. I'm serious."

"It's the truth I'm telling you, Edwin Michael James!"

"But you don't *look* anything like the Devil," Edwin challenged. "Where are your horns? Your cloven feet? Your spiked tail?"

"Oh, *really*," the man said in a rather bored way. "I was, after all, once an angel. But if you *insist*." There was another black flash, and before him stood the Devil, just as Edwin always imagined he would look. He was a red, hairy fellow with cloven hooves, tail, and horns. The Devil still held the oak case.

"Can I offer you a drink?" Edwin held out his jug.

"When was it made?" the Devil asked.

"Last night. It was the last thing I did before going to bed."

The Devil grimaced. "But doesn't age improve corn whiskey?"

"I don't know who told you that," Edwin chuckled. "I once kept a batch around for a whole week one time, and I couldn't say that it was a bit fresher or better-tasting than when it was first made. So take it and drink, and if you don't mind my asking, what brings you 'round these parts?"

The Devil took a long swig and nearly choked. He handed it back to Edwin and in a wheezing voice said, "Smooth as silk." Then he looked the moonshiner in the eye, "You aren't afraid of me, are you, Edwin James?"

Ed sniffed at the jug. It smelled like wet earth and sulphur. He discreetly wiped it with his coat sleeve before taking another draught. "I can't say as I have any reason to be. I've been to Mass and I've said my prayers."

They passed the bottle around a few more times and both were soon half-drunk. The Devil was carelessly breathing out fire, and Edwin had to swat out a few sparks that landed on the pitch-tar roof of his cabin. "Watch it, now! My wife and kids are in there!"

"Sorry," the Devil mumbled. "But, say, Edwin, did you know I'm a piper, too?"

"Go on!"

"It's God's own truth I'm telling you!"

"That's blasphemy, sir!"

"Sorry," the Devil mumbled again. "I sometimes forget. But I'm serious. How about us having a piping contest?"

"All right," agreed Edwin.

The Devil opened up his case. "I'll start us off then."

"Funny how you just happened to bring your pipes," Edwin remarked drily.

The Devil strapped his pipes around his waist. Fire flew from his fingertips as he practiced a few scales.

"Ready?" asked Edwin.

"Ready!" said the Devil. He played a slow air first, and it was so eerie that shivers ran up and down Edwin's spine. Then the Devil launched into a jig, and with a band of goblins that had appeared from nowhere, finished off with a reel.

"Well," said Edwin as he looked at the Devil's smug face. "You're pretty good. But say, we never set a wager."

"Oh," sniffed the Devil nonchalantly. "How about we battle for your soul?"

"You get right to it, don't you? And if I win?"

"Why!" beamed the Devil. "You can have my pipes; a finer set you'll never own."

"They are mighty sweet." Edwin eyed them critically. "Okay, it's a deal, although it's probably a sin and you'll get my soul anyway." Then he played his own pipes, the ones his grandfather had given him, and the angels must have been smiling on him despite his arrogance, for he played hornpipes, jigs, and reels better than the Prince of Darkness.

The Devil could hardly believe his ears, but he was a gracious loser. He set the pipes on the ground at Edwin's feet. "Although it burns me to be beaten by a mortal, I have to admit you're the finest piper I've heard on either side of the ocean." Then he sank into the earth and was gone.

"Wait!" shouted Edwin. "Take a jug of the spirits with you! As a token of good will!"

"Keep it!" the Devil's head popped up from the earth. "It's warm enough down here as it is, and I'm already sure of getting a nasty hangover from your rotgut."

"Suit yourself," Edwin grinned, and went inside with both sets of pipes. He tried to get into bed, but his wife had other ideas.

"You reek of moonshine and smoke! You've had an accident with the still, haven't you? Well! You're not coming in here, stinking up the bedclothes as you are!"

Edwin stood alone in the front yard. "A bath?" he asked incredulously. "She wants me to take a bath?!?"

And so that is the tale, as it is told in the Appalachians, of the time Edwin James gave the Devil his due, and how the Devil got his revenge.

8.
THE ANIMAL KINGDOM

Fine Words Butter No Parsnips

———————◆❋◆———————

THERE WAS A BLACKSMITH in Skibbereen who lived there long before the English settled there, and people would travel many a mile for his fine work. These people irritated the smith, however, for no matter what task he did for them, great or small, they would only give him a "God spare you your health," in payment.

"It's a very nice prayer, *God spare you your health,*" the smith would sarcastically say to his wife. "But it does not buy us a loaf of bread or a flitch of bacon at the market. They expect me to give them hard currency."

Prayers, no matter how kindly they were offered, would not feed his family. It would drive him mad when one of his customers would say, "God spare you your health," but he never said anything back to them.

One day he had had enough, however, and when the first customer of the day said, "Thank you smith, God spare you your health," he replied with "Oh, let my dog have that blessing."

His dog sat in the corner of the smithy, and whenever someone had no payment for the smith other than a blessing, he would bestow that blessing on the wolfhound. No other food or drink would he give it, not even water, and it wasn't long before the dog was dead.

A woman came into the smithy with a pair of scissors she wanted sharpened, and the smith did them a good turn so that they could cut through the heaviest of cloth. The woman beamed her appreciation, and then said, "God spare you your health," before turning to leave.

Instead of answering, "Amen, and also to you," the

smith said, "Look over at my dog in the corner. He is not sleeping, he is dead. If prayers could feed a creature, then he should be hale and strong, for every prayer I've been given I've bestowed upon him. Do you understand my meaning?"

"Indeed I do, smith," the woman blushed furiously. She reached into her purse and asked, "What would the sharpening cost me?"

It wasn't long before the news of the smith's dog spread throughout the village of Skibbereen, and ever afterward the people would say, "God spare you your health, smith, and what would that be costing me?"

Kieran & the Little Bird

ONCE ON A TIME, long, and long, and very long ago, there lived a religious and holy man known as Kieran. Kieran was one of the monks of a monastery, and he loved nothing better than to work outdoors. So it happened one day that as he was tending the cabbages in the garden, he heard a bird singing in one of the abbot's rose trees.

"Never before have I heard such sweet music," Kieran thought to himself as he rose from his knees to listen to the bird's song. "Never before have I heard such a heavenly voice."

When the little bird had finished its song, it flew to a tree on the other side of the monastery. There it began to sing anew. The monk put down his spade and followed the bird, intent on hearing more of its wonderful music.

After that the little bird flew to another distant tree, and sung there for a while, and then on to another tree, and so on and so on, further and further away from the monastery. Kieran continued to follow, listening in delight and wonder to the tiny creature.

Finally, the monk knew that he could not neglect his duties any longer, and he decided to return for the evening prayers. When he came into the monastery grounds, he was amazed at everything he saw. Not one face was familiar to him. Indeed, the buildings themselves seemed strangely altered, and the garden he tended was no longer where he thought it should be.

While he stood, confused and dazed, one of the monks of the convent came up to join him, and Kieran asked, "My brother, what has happened here? What is the meaning of all of these changes? I don't understand how this could have happened since morning."

The monk that he spoke to stared at him in surprise. "Whatever are you talking about, my friend? Sure it is that everything is the same as when I awoke."

"You are wrong," said Kieran emphatically. "Even my cabbage patch is gone."

"Brother," said the other monk. "What is your name? Why do you ask such odd questions? I can tell from your habit that you are a man of our order, but I know that I have never before seen your face."

So Kieran told the monk his name, and said that he had been working in the garden only that morning before he had wandered away to hear the bird's song.

"Kieran?" the other man asked. "You say your name is Kieran? There is a legend told at this monastery of a brother by the name of Kieran."

"And what does this legend say?"

The monk was silent for a moment, then he quietly said, "The story tells how he had disappeared over two hundred years ago, and how he was never seen again."

"Blessed be the name of the Lord," said Kieran. "And blessed be the name of His son Jesus Christ. The hour of my death has come." He kneeled before the other monk and said, "My friend, can you take my confession? I feel that my soul is departing."

And so Kieran made his confession, and received absolution, and was anointed, and died.

The little bird, don't you know, was an angel sent from heaven; that was the way in which the Lord chose to take to Himself the soul of the holy man.

Saint Ciaran & the Animals

T HE FIRST OF THE SAINTS to be born in Ireland and to be of Irish blood was Saint Ciaran, and that blood was the noble blood of Leinster. The very first of the miracles he was to perform was on the Isle of Cleire, and he but a young lad not yet ten.

While he was walking along in the countryside, there came a hawk swooping over his head, and it snatched up a little bird that was flying before Ciaran. The young boy pitied the bird, and he said aloud, "Fly away, hawk, and leave this creature of God alone." Lo and behold! The hawk dropped the sparrow at his feet and flew away.

The poor little creature was trembling and half-dead, but Ciaran picked him up and said, "Arise, little one, in the name of God." And rise the bird did, and flew back safely to its nest.

Saint Patrick himself heard of this miracle, and he told Ciaran, "Go to the Well of Uaran, where the north meets the south in the middle of Ireland, and carry with you my bell. You are not to speak until you arrive there safely."

So Ciaran did as he was told, and when he reached the holy well the bell spoke in pure, clear tones, "You are here, my faithful one."

Ciaran set up camp where he was, alone in the great woods, and he built for himself a little hut.

The first disciple that Ciaran had was a wild boar. It came into his cell as meek as a lamb, and said to Ciaran, "I will help make your home more sturdy." Every day he went into the woods to dig up thatch and sticks.

Many more wild animals came to Ciaran, including a fox and a badger, a wolf and a doe, and they said to him,

"Teach us about the Holy Trinity."

The fox, however, could never really be trusted. He was, by nature, greedy and cunning and full of spite, and he snatched Ciaran's shoes when he wasn't wearing them. Ciaran, being a saint, knew what was going on, and he had the badger fetch the shoes back.

Ciaran said to the fox, "My brother, how could you betray me so? There was no need for you to steal my shoes; if you wanted to wear shoes, I would have made them for you."

The fox refused to mend his ways, and was cast out from the community. To this day a fox cannot be trusted, and can be expected to look out for himself only.

The Cuckoo of Spring

THE SEVENTH OF APRIL is the feast of Saint Brynach, and each year, as far back as people can recall, it is also the day when the first cuckoo of spring arrives at the Church of Nevern to perch on the tall Celtic cross dedicated to the saint. Saint Brynach had a great love and understanding of animals, and it was believed by the townspeople that the cuckoo's annual journey was a religious obligation in memory of the holy man. It became the custom that the priest of Nevern would not begin Mass on Saint Brynach's Day until the cuckoo had arrived.

But it happened one year that the winter was particularly long and harsh, and when the seventh of April came around, there was no sign of the cuckoo or of spring. The ground was still too frozen to plow, and there was not a single blossom or bud on the trees. Just the same, the people of Nevern gathered outside the church to await the arrival of God's messenger. Hour after long hour they waited, huddled beneath the great cross, and still there was no sign of the tiny bird. Midday came and went, and the people became cold and tired.

"Perhaps we should give up and go home," said one old man, blowing on his icy hands.

"Not without celebrating Mass," replied a young mother. "We can still go inside and hear the service."

But the priest would not listen to any of them, and he said, "God cares for all his creatures, great and small, and he will not let the cuckoo fail. We will wait here a while longer."

The sun began to sink towards the horizon, and in the fading twilight the congregation heard a slight fluttering of wings in the nearby trees. "Blessed be," the people whispered to each other. "God has not forgotten us."

The weary little bird landed on the very top of Saint Brynach's Cross and warbled a weak *cuck-oo, cuck-oo.* Spring had finally arrived.

"Now we can go inside," the priest beamed, and the people crowded into the church to hear the much awaited Mass.

When they came back outside, they found the cuckoo dead at the foot of the ancient stone cross. The long, harsh journey across the frozen mountains of Europe and the storm-tossed waters of the Channel had taken their toll. But the tiny creature had kept its trust, and with much reverence was buried below the saint's memorial.

9.
CRIMINALS
AND SINNERS

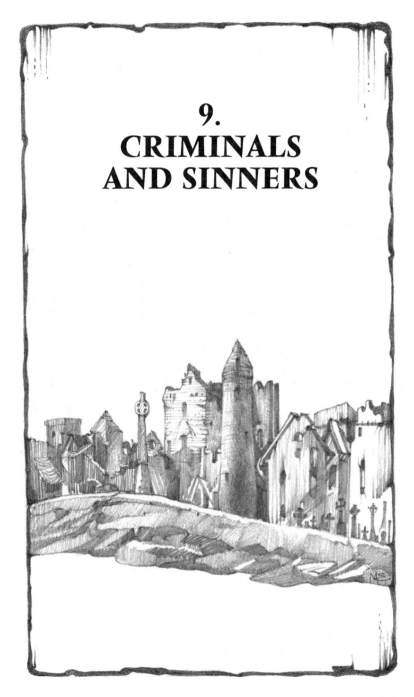

The Sunbeam

THERE WAS A poor man named Douglas MacConmara who was at one time working for a farmer in the Wicklow Mountains, and the job he had was tending the cattle. He was away from home for so much of the time that it was seldom he made it to Mass. Nevertheless, he was a very devout man. When Mass was going on in the village, he would kneel in the field among his cattle with his hat in his hands, facing the direction of the chapel to say his prayers.

One Sunday the farmer sent his little son to tend the cattle, and Douglas was able to go to town. It was a bitterly cold day, and he pulled his old coat tightly around his shoulders. But when he was down from the mountain it grew quite warm, and he took off his coat and carried it instead. When he got inside the chapel, he laid the coat down beside him, and where did it rest but on a sunbeam shining in through the stained-glass window. The sunbeam actually held the coat up!

When the priest stood at the pulpit, he spied the coat and he thought to himself, "Why, this is a very holy man! Why else would the coat remain like that?" After the service he sought out the poor man, and urged him to attend Mass every Sunday. "I'll even send one of my altar boys to watch the cattle for you," he said.

So Douglas went to church every Sunday from then on, and every Sunday he hung up his coat on a sunbeam.

As he went to church, Douglas would sometimes listen to others chatting on the road, and you can believe it wasn't always Christian charity that they were discussing. Oftentimes they would cruelly criticize their neighbors and spread idle gossip. One day he was listening to two

middle-aged sisters tearing apart the character of another woman, and he found himself nodding along in agreement. "She must be a right *srimileál* with all that talk about her!"

And when he went to church, he laid his coat across the sunbeam, and it fell right to the floor. The priest noticed this, and afterwards he questioned Douglas on the matter. "What sin did you commit?" he asked. When he heard about the gossip, he said, "That is a sin worse than stealing. I'll give you absolution, but you must promise not to listen to that kind of talk again."

The very next Sunday, Douglas MacConmara was able to hang his coat on the sunbeam, as he was every Sunday after that.

Saint Peter & Saint Fachtna

SAINT PETER, having grown weary of opening and shutting the Gates of Heaven all day long, fervently wished to visit the jewel of Ireland, Carrick-an-Sur, and asked Saint Fachtna if he would take his place for a while.

Saint Fachtna was a kindly soul, always willing to help out if there was a need, and he cheerfully agreed. "I've always thought it would be fun to stand guard at the Pearly Gates," he said. He listened carefully as Saint Peter explained the mechanisms of the gate, promising to not refuse admittance to those who knocked, and to patiently answer all questions, no matter how ridiculous they might sound.

Saint Peter was about to leave for his trip when Saint Fachtna suddenly grabbed hold of his gown. "Wait, Peter! What happens if an Englishman should knock at the gate? I don't know *one word* of English."

"No danger of that happening, surely!" laughed Saint Peter. "You needn't trouble yourself at all with worrying. Many a century has passed since I first took charge of these gates, and although people of almost every nation have knocked, no Englishman has yet appeared to seek entrance."

Then Saint Peter left, and for a while Saint Fachtna undertook the job of gatekeeper. Although he was called upon to answer all sorts of odd questions, not once did he have to strain his tongue, for no Englishman ever knocked on the Gates of Heaven.

The Cursed Well of Ballintober

'TIS A LEE and a long while now since this story took place, and all the people who witnessed these events have been in their graves for a thousand years.

There used to be a holy well in the town of Ballintober. Folks said that on its site there once stood a monastery. Where the altar of the chapel was, a well of spring water broke through, and it was known as Mary's Well. A beautiful white dove landed nearby, and spoke with the words of human speech, "Never will a blind man visit this well but would get his sight."

There was a man named Darby who lived near the well and who didn't believe a word of the miracle. "Stuff and nonsense!" he snorted. "Nothing in it but tricks and *pishtrogues* to fool the people!" To prove his point he brought a blind donkey to the well and stuck its head under the blessed spring. Lo and behold! The ass regained his sight, but Darby lost his.

Every good thing is eventually spoiled by some evil-doer, and Mary's Well is no different. A young girl of Ballintober was to soon be married, and as she was trying on her wedding clothes an old blind woman came to her door, begging alms in the name of God and Mary. "I have nothing to give you, you worthless old woman," the girl spat. "It's bothered I am that you darken my door. Be gone with you, now!"

The old woman's face went purple with rage, and she shouted, "May your sweetheart never place the wedding band on your finger until you are as blind as I am!"

Instantly the girl was struck blind. Going to Mary's

Well to be cured, she encountered the old woman. "You again?" she shrieked. "Get out of my way!"

The girl and the old woman fell to quarrelling and knocking each other about, and both of them tumbled into the holy well and were drowned. From that day onward the waters were cursed, and no one has ever been cured by them again.

The Power of Prayer

A VERY OLD WOMAN, Maeve O'Reilly, used to travel up and down the roads of County Mayo, asking for alms. The only prayer she knew was a short one, but she said it often:

> "God bless to me this day,
> God bless to me this night;
> Bless, O bless, Thou God of grace,
> Each day and hour of my life."

She reached a farmhouse one evening, and asked the farmer for lodging for the night. The farmer readily agreed, and she was shown to a room next to the kitchen.

Now this particular farmer had three sons, all of whom were thieves. He was constantly praying that they would mend their evil ways and choose a more spiritual path.

The three brothers planned to murder the old woman as she slept and steal what few possessions she had. The first one went to the door of her room and looked in through the keyhole. He saw standing next to the bed a guardian angel dressed in a shining gown of white and holding a flaming sword. "I'm not going in there!" he whispered.

"What do you mean?" asked the second brother as he, too, peered in the keyhole. He saw two angels guarding the bed, one with a flaming sword and one with a crystal shield. "I'm not stepping one foot in there, either!" he shouted.

"Hush!" said the third brother. "You'll wake the whole house!" He peered through the keyhole, and he saw three guardian angels! The first carried a flaming sword, the second carried a crystal shield, and the third carried a cross of gold.

"I think it is a sign," said the first brother, "a sign to give up our thieving ways."

And so the boys did so, and for the first time in many a year, were seen at Mass that Sunday.

Friar Killian & the Devil's Bargain

———◆❋◆———

L ONG, AND LONG, and long ago there lived a carefree young man named Finn who had a great love for horses, whiskey, and gambling. He sent himself deep into debt, and did not know how he was going to pay off his bills.

As he was heading home from the pub one night, he met a man who said to him, "I often see you walking down this road."

"Is there a reason you're telling me this?" said Finn sharply. "It's soon enough that you'll see me here all the time. I spent my last shilling on a pint of stout."

"Hear now," said the man, "I can give you all the money you want—in sterling—if you will give to me a contract saying that you're mine at the end of twenty-one years.

"The Devil dances in an empty pocket, isn't that what the people say?" asked Finn sadly. "You are the Devil in the guise of a man, are you not?"

"I am, and will you sign a contract with me?"

"I will."

"Be sure to sign it in blood," added the Devil.

For one and twenty years Finn had money any time he needed it, but when the end of his contract approached, a great fear took hold of him. He went to the priest of his parish and told him the whole story. "What will become of me?" asked Finn. "It's a mess I've made of my life, there's no doubt."

"I haven't had many dealings with the Devil," said the

priest. "But my friend Friar Killian has, and perhaps he can help you."

So Finn went to Friar Killian and told him the entire sad tale. The friar thought a moment, and then said, "Here is a rowan stick for you. You must draw a circle on the ground with this stick, and you should be standing within the circle as you do so. The Devil won't be able to touch you while you're there."

"I can't say within the circle forever," said Finn. "Eventually the Devil will get hold of me."

"I only want you to get him talking; then tell him that you want a judgment in the matter. I'll be with you, hidden, but able to hear all."

So Finn did as the friar instructed, and the Devil found him within a magic circle. "Come along now," he said to Finn. "It's time we completed our bargain."

"It's a judgment I want, and I won't leave until I have it."

"Oh, very well," the Devil said impatiently. "Then we'll let the first person who walks by decide the matter."

Just then Friar Killian stepped up, agreeing to act as judge. "Now, tell me from the beginning, what this matter's all about."

The Devil told him how he had bought the soul of this man twenty-one years ago, and how he had now come to collect that soul.

Friar Killian thought a moment and said, "If you were to go to the trading fair to buy a horse or a cow, and if you paid earnest money for that beast, wouldn't you say it was more proper for you to have the animal than for some chap who would come that night and who would buy it without any earnest money?"

"That's clear," said the Devil. "The man who paid earnest money for it ought to get it."

"Just as the Son of God paid earnest money for this lad here before you bought him."

"You tricked me, so you did!" spat the Devil, disappearing into a cloud of green smoke.

"The great deceiver is himself tricked in the end," laughed Friar Killian. Then he turned to Finn and said, "I think it's a trip to the church we should be making now, don't you agree?"

"Most wholeheartedly," said Finn.

Index